A·LITTLE·BOOK·OF PRAYERS·AND·HYMNS

The reproductions in this book have been made using the most modern electronic scanning methods from entirely new transparencies of Cicely Mary Barker's original watercolours. They enable Cicely Mary Barker's skill as an artist to be appreciated as never before.

FREDERICK WARNE
Published by the Penguin Group
Penguin Books Ltd, 27 Wrights Lane, London W8 5TZ, England
Penguin Books USA Inc., 375 Hudson Street, New York, N.Y. 10014, USA
Penguin Books Australia Ltd, Ringwood, Victoria, Australia
Penguin Books Canada Ltd, 10 Alcorn Avenue, Toronto, Ontario, Canada M4V 3B2
Penguin Books (N.Z.) Ltd, 182-190 Wairau Road, Auckland 10, New Zealand

Penguin Books Ltd, Registered Offices: Harmondsworth, Middlesex, England

First published 1994
5 7 9 10 8 6 4

Universal Copyright Notice:
Text and original illustrations copyright © The Estate of
Cicely Mary Barker, 1923, 1926, 1934, 1940, 1944, 1948
New reproductions copyright © The Estate of Cicely Mary Barker, 1994
This presentation copyright © The Estate of Cicely Mary Barker, 1994
Copyright in all countries signatory to the Berne Convention

All rights reserved. Without limiting the rights under copyright reserved above, no part of this publication may be reproduced, stored in or introduced into a retrieval system, or transmitted, in any form or by any means (electronic, mechanical, photocopying, recording or otherwise), without the prior written permission of both the copyright owner and the above publisher of this book.

ISBN 0 7232 4109 0

Colour reproduction by Saxon
Printed and bound in Great Britain by
William Clowes Limited, Beccles and London

A·LITTLE·BOOK OF·PRAYERS AND·HYMNS

Chosen, illustrated and decorated by
CICELY MARY BARKER

———◆———

FREDERICK WARNE

✦CONTENTS✦

We Plough the Fields   11
M. Claudius

Grace Before Meat   12

The King of Love   14
Henry Williams Baker

Onward, Christian Soldiers   17
Sabine Baring-Gould

The Lord's My Shepherd   20
David Grant

Love Divine   23
Charles Wesley

Praise to the Lord, the Almighty   24
Joachim Neander

Dear Lord and Father of Mankind   27
J.G. Whittier

All Glory, Laud and Honour   29
St Theodulph of Orleans

Littles   32
Robert Herrick

Christ the Lord is Risen Again   35
Michael Weisse

The Lamb   36
William Blake

A Great and Mighty Wonder   39
St. Germanus

On Christmas Day in the Morning   41

O Come, All Ye Faithful   43

Another Grace   45
Robert Herrick

Away in a Manger   47

While Shepherds Watched   48
Nahum Tate

He Prayeth Well   51
Samuel Taylor Coleridge

The Shepherd Boy's Song   53
John Bunyan

All Things Bright and Beautiful   54
C.F. Alexander

Christmas Carol   57

Prayer at Bedtime   58

We Plough the Fields

WE PLOUGH THE FIELDS

We plough the fields and scatter
   The good seed on the land,
But it is fed and watered
   By God's almighty hand;
He sends the snow in winter,
   The warmth to swell the grain,
The breezes and the sunshine,
   And soft refreshing rain.
All good gifts around us
   Are sent from Heav'n above,
Then thank the Lord,
   O thank the Lord,
For all His love.

He only is the Maker
   Of all things near and far;
He paints the wayside flower;
   He lights the evening star;
The winds and waves obey Him;
   By Him the birds are fed;
Much more to us, His children,
   He gives our daily bread.
All good gifts, etc.

GRACE BEFORE MEAT
Three Very Old Graces

I

Bless these Thy gifts, most gracious God,
    From whom all goodness springs;
Make clean our hearts and feed our souls
    With good and joyful things.

II

Pray we to God, the Almighty Lord,
    That sendeth food to beasts and men,
To send His blessing on this board,
    To feed us now and ever. Amen.

III

God bless our meat,
God guide our ways,
God give us grace
Our Lord to please.
Lord, long preserve in peace and health
Our gracious Queen Elizabeth.

Grace Before Meat

THE KING OF LOVE

The King of Love my Shepherd is,
    Whose goodness faileth never;
I nothing lack if I am His
    And He is mine forever.

Where streams of living water flow
    My ransomed soul He leadeth,
And, where the verdant pastures grow,
    With food celestial feedeth.

Perverse and foolish oft I strayed,
    But yet in love He sought me,
And on His shoulder gently laid,
    And home, rejoicing, brought me.

In death's dark vale I fear no ill
    With Thee, dear Lord, beside me;
Thy rod and staff my comfort still,
    Thy Cross before to guide me.

The King of Love

Thou spread'st a table in my sight;
    Thy unction grace bestoweth:
And oh, what transport of delight
    From Thy pure chalice floweth!

And so through all the length of days
    Thy goodness faileth never:
Good Shepherd, may I sing Thy praise
    Within Thy house for ever.

ONWARD, CHRISTIAN SOLDIERS

Onward, Christian soldiers,
   Marching as to war,
With the cross of Jesus
   Going on before.
Christ, the Royal Master,
   Leads against the foe;
Forward into battle,
   See, His banners go!
Onward, Christian soldiers,
   Marching as to war,
With the cross of Jesus
   Going on before.

At the sign of triumph
   Satan's host doth flee;
On then, Christian soldiers,
   On to victory!
Hell's foundations quiver
   At the shout of praise;
Brothers, lift your voices,
   Loud your anthems raise.

Onward, Christian Soldiers

Onward, Christian, etc.

Like a mighty army
    Moves the Church of God;
Brothers, we are treading
    Where the saints have trod;
We are not divided,
    All one body we,
One in hope and doctrine,
    One in charity.
Onward, Christian, etc.

THE LORD'S MY SHEPHERD

The Lord's my shepherd, I'll not want.
    He makes me down to lie
In pastures green; He leadeth me
    The quiet waters by.

My soul He doth restore again;
    And me to walk doth make
Within the paths of righteousness,
    E'en for His own name's sake.

Yea, though I walk in death's dark vale,
    Yet will I fear none ill;
For Thou art with me, and Thy rod
    And staff me comfort still.

My table Thou hast furnished
    In presence of my foes;
My head thou dost with oil anoint,
    And my cup overflows.

The Lord's My Shepherd

Love Divine

LOVE DIVINE

Love divine, all loves excelling,
   Joy of heaven to earth come down,
Fix in us Thy humble dwelling,
   All Thy faithful mercies crown.

Jesus, Thou art all compassion,
   Pure, unbounded love Thou art;
Visit us with Thy salvation,
   Enter ev'ry trembling heart.

Come, Almighty, to deliver,
   Let us all Thy life receive;
Come to us, dear Lord, and never,
   Never more Thy temples leave.

Thee we would be always blessing;
   Serve Thee as Thy hosts above;
Pray, and praise Thee without ceasing;
   Glory in Thy perfect love.

PRAISE TO THE LORD, THE ALMIGHTY

Praise to the Lord, the Almighty, the King of creation!
O my soul, praise Him, for He is your health and salvation.
All you who hear, now to His altar draw near,
Join in profound adoration.

Praise to the Lord, let us offer our gifts at His altar;
Let not our sins and transgressions now cause us to falter.
Christ, the High Priest, bids us all join in His feast,
Victims with Him on the altar.

Praise to the Lord, oh, let all that is in us adore Him!
All that has life and breath, come now in praises before Him.
Let the Amen sound from His people again,
Now as we worship before Him.

Praise To the Lord, the Almighty

Dear Lord and Father of Mankind

DEAR LORD AND FATHER OF MANKIND

Dear Lord and Father of mankind,
  Forgive our foolish ways!
Re-clothe us in our rightful mind,
  In purer lives Thy service find,
In deeper reverence praise.
  In deeper reverence praise.

In simple trust like theirs who heard,
  Beside the Syrian sea,
The gracious calling of the Lord,
  Let us, like them, without a word
 Rise up and follow Thee.
  Rise up and follow Thee.

O Sabbath rest by Galilee!
  O calm of hills above,
Where Jesus knelt to share with Thee
  The silence of eternity,
Interpreted by love!
  Interpreted by love!

Drop Thy still dews of quietness,
   Till all our strivings cease;
Take from our souls the strain and stress,
   And let our ordered lives confess
The beauty of Thy peace.
   The beauty of Thy peace.

Breathe through the heats of our desire
   Thy coolness and Thy balm;
Let sense be dumb, let flesh retire;
   Speak through the earthquake, wind, and fire,
O still small voice of calm!
   O still small voice of calm!

ALL GLORY, LAUD AND HONOUR

All glory, laud, and honour
  To Thee, Redeemer, King,
To Whom the lips of children
  Made sweet Hosannas ring!
Thou art the King of Israel,
  Thou David's Royal Son,
Who in the Lord's name comest,
  The King and Blessèd One.

All glory, laud, and honour
  To Thee, Redeemer, King,
To Whom the lips of children
  Made sweet Hosannas ring!
The company of angels
  Are praising Thee on high,
And mortal men, and all things
  Created make reply.

All glory, laud, and honour
  To Thee, Redeemer, King,
To Whom the lips of children
  Made sweet Hosannas ring!
The people of the Hebrews
  With palms before Thee went,
Our praise and prayer and anthems
  Before Thee we present.

All glory, laud, and honour
  To Thee, Redeemer, King,
To Whom the lips of children
  Made sweet Hosannas ring!
To Thee before Thy Passion
  They sang their hymns of praise;
To Thee now high exalted
  Our melody we raise.

All Glory, Laud and Honour

LITTLES
(From "A Ternarie of Littles")

A little Saint best fits
   a little Shrine,
As little Prop best fits
   a little Vine,
As my small Cruse best
   fits my little Wine.

A little Seed best fits a little Soil,
A little Trade best fits a little Toil,
As my small Jar best fits my little Oil.

A little Bin best fits a little Bread,
A little Garland fits a little Head,
As my small Stuff best fits my little Shed.

A little Hearth best
  fits a little Fire,
A little Chapel best
  fits a little Choir,
As my small Bell best
  fits my little Spire.

A little Stream best fits a little Boat,
A little Lead best fits a little Float,
As my small Pipe best fits my little Note.

Christ the Lord is Risen Again

CHRIST THE LORD IS RISEN AGAIN

Christ the Lord is risen again; *Alleluya!*
Christ hath broken every chain; *Alleluya!*
Hark, angelic voices cry, *Alleluya!*
Singing evermore on high *Alleluya!*

He Who bore all pain and loss, *Alleluya!*
Comfortless upon the Cross, *Alleluya!*
Lives in glory now on high, *Alleluya!*
Pleads for us and hears our cry; *Alleluya!*

Thou, our Paschal Lamb indeed, *Alleluya!*
Christ, Thy ransomed people feed: *Alleluya!*
Take our sins and guilt away, *Alleluya!*
Let us sing by night and day, *Alleluya!*

THE LAMB

Little Lamb, who made thee?
Dost thou know who made thee,
Gave thee life, and bade thee feed
By the stream and o'er the mead;
Gave thee clothing of delight,
Softest clothing, woolly, bright;
Gave thee such a tender voice,
Making all the vales rejoice?
Little Lamb, who made thee?
Dost thou know who made thee?

    Little Lamb, I'll tell thee,
    Little Lamb, I'll tell thee;
He is callèd by thy name,
For He calls Himself a Lamb.
He is meek, and He is mild,
He became a little child.
I a child, and thou a lamb,
We are callèd by His name.
    Little Lamb, God Bless thee!
    Little Lamb, God bless thee!

A Great and Mighty Wonder

A GREAT AND MIGHTY WONDER

A great and mighty wonder,
  A full and holy cure!
The Virgin bears the Infant
  With virgin-honour pure.
Repeat the hymn again!
  "To God on high be glory,
And peace on earth to men!"

The Word becomes incarnate
  And yet remains on high!
And Cherubim sing anthems
  To shepherds from the sky.
Repeat the hymn, etc.

While thus they sing your Monarch,
  Those bright angelic bands,
Rejoice, ye vales and mountains,
  Ye oceans clap your hands.
Repeat the hymn, etc.

Since all He comes to ransom,
  By all be He adored,
The Infant born in Bethl'em,
  The Saviour and the Lord.
Repeat the hymn, etc.

ON CHRISTMAS DAY IN THE MORNING
(From the Carol "I Saw Three Ships")

And all the bells on earth shall ring,
    On Christmas Day, on Christmas Day,
And all the bells on earth shall ring
    On Christmas Day in the morning.

And all the Angels in heaven shall sing,
    On Christmas Day, on Christmas Day,
And all the Angels in heaven shall sing
    On Christmas Day in the morning.

And all the souls on earth shall sing,
    On Christmas Day, on Christmas Day,
And all the souls on earth shall sing
    On Christmas Day in the morning.

Then let us all rejoice amain,
    On Christmas Day, on Christmas Day,
Then let us all rejoice amain
    On Christmas Day in the morning.

O Come, All Ye Faithful

O COME, ALL YE FAITHFUL

O come, all ye faithful,
  Joyful and triumphant;
O come ye, O come ye to Bethlehem;
  Come and behold Him
Born the King of Angels;
  O come, let us adore Him,
O come, let us adore Him,
  O come, let us adore Him,
Christ the Lord.

God of God,
  Light of Light,
Lo! He abhors not the Virgin's womb;
  Very God,
Begotten, not created;
  O come, let us adore Him, etc.

Sing, choirs of angels,
  Sing in exultation,
Sing, all ye citizens of heaven above,
  Glory to God
In the highest;
  O come, let us adore Him, etc.

Yea, Lord, we greet Thee,
  Born this happy morning;
Jesu, to Thee be glory given;
  Word of the Father,
Now in flesh appearing;
  O come, let us adore Him, etc.

ANOTHER GRACE

What God gives, and what we take,
'Tis a gift for Christ His sake:
Be the meal of Beans and Pease
God be thanked for those, and these:
Have we flesh, or have we fish,
All are Fragments from His dish.

Away in a Manger

AWAY IN A MANGER

Away in a manger, no crib for a bed,
  The little Lord Jesus lay down His sweet head,
The stars in the bright sky looked down where
    He lay,
  The little Lord Jesus asleep on the hay.

The cattle are lowing, the Baby awakes,
  But little Lord Jesus no crying He makes.
I love Thee, Lord Jesus! look down from the sky,
  And stay by my side until morning is nigh.

Be near me, Lord Jesus; I ask Thee to stay
  Close by me for ever, and love me, I pray.
Bless all the dear children in Thy tender care,
  And fit us for heaven, to live with Thee there.

WHILE SHEPHERDS WATCHED

While shepherds watched their flocks by night,
  All seated on the ground,
The angel of the Lord came down,
  And glory shone around.

"Fear not," said he; for mighty dread
  Had seized their troubled mind;
"Glad tidings of great joy I bring
  To you and all mankind.

"To you in David's town this day
  Is born of David's line
A Saviour, Who is Christ the Lord:
  And this shall be the sign:

"The heavenly Babe you there shall find
  To human view displayed,
All meanly wrapped in swathing bands,
  And in a manger laid."

While Shepherds Watched

Thus spake the seraph; and forthwith
  Appeared a shining throng
Of angels praising God, who thus
  Addressed their joyful song:

"All glory be to God on high,
  And in the earth be peace;
Goodwill henceforth from Heaven to men
  Begin and never cease."

HE PRAYETH WELL

He prayeth well, who loveth well
  Both man and bird and beast.
He prayeth best, who loveth best
  All things both great and small;
For the dear God who loveth us,
  He made and loveth all.

The Shepherd Boy's Song

THE SHEPHERD BOY'S SONG

He that is down needs fear no fall,
  He that is low, no pride;
He that is humble ever shall
  Have God to be his guide.

I am content with what I have,
  Little be it or much:
And, Lord, contentment still I crave,
  Because thou savest such.

Fulness to such a burden is
  That goes on pilgrimage:
Here little, and hereafter bliss,
  Is best from age to age.

ALL THINGS BRIGHT AND BEAUTIFUL

All things bright and beautiful,
  All creatures great and small,
All things wise and wonderful,
  The Lord God made them all.

Each little flow'r that opens,
  Each little bird that sings,
He made their glowing colours,
  He made their tiny wings.

All things bright and beautiful, etc.

The purple-headed mountain,
  The river running by,
The sunset, and the morning
  That brightens up the sky;

All things bright and beautiful, etc.

The cold wind in the winter,
  The pleasant summer sun,
The ripe fruits in the garden,
  He made them every one;

All Things Bright and Beautiful

All things bright and beautiful, etc.

The tall trees in the greenwood,
   The meadows where we play,
The rushes by the water,
   We gather every day;

All things bright and beautiful, etc.

He gave us eyes to see them,
   And lips that we might tell,
How great is God Almighty,
   Who has made all things well.

All things bright and beautiful,
   All creatures great and small,
All things wise and wonderful,
   The Lord God made them all.

CHRISTMAS CAROL

The snow lay on the ground,
  the star shone bright,
When Christ our Lord was born
  on Christmas night,
When Christ our Lord was born
  on Christmas night.

'Twas Mary, daughter pure of Holy Ann,
That brought Him to this world,
  our Lord made man,
That brought Him to this world,
  our Lord made man.

She laid Him on the straw at Bethlehem,
The ass and oxen shared the roof
  with them,
The ass and oxen shared the roof
  with them.

PRAYER AT BEDTIME

Matthew, Mark, Luke, and John,
Bless the bed that I lie on.
Four corners to my bed,
Four Angels there be spread:
One at the head, one at the feet,
And two to guard me while I sleep.
God within, and God without,
And Jesus Christ all round about;
If any danger come to me,
Sweet Jesus Christ deliver me.
Before I lay me down to sleep
I give my soul to Christ to keep;
And if I die before I wake,
I pray that Christ my soul will take.

Prayer at Bedtime